GREAT PICTURES

AND THEIR STORIES

How To Look At Pictures

"You must look at pictures studiously, earnestly, honestly. It will take years before you come to a full appreciation of art; but when at last you have it, you will be possessed of the purest, loftiest and most ennobling pleasures that the civilized world can offer you."

JOHN C. VAN DYKE.

ST.
AA
PRESS

GREAT PICTURES
᠃THEIR STORIES

INTERPRETING
MASTERPIECES
TO CHILDREN

BY
KATHERINE MORRIS LESTER

BOOK EIGHT

St. Augustine Academy Press

This book was originally published in 1927
by Mentzer, Bush & Company.

This facsimile edition reprinted in 2024
with improved color images
by St. Augustine Academy Press.

ISBN: 978-1-64051-151-4

CONTENTS

Page

George Washington (Gibbs-Channing) ....*Stuart* 13

Upon the Stairs................*Zorn* 25

Cotopaxi ....*Church* 33

Syndics of the Cloth Guild.......*Rembrandt* .. 45

An Arrangement in Black and Gray ....*Whistler* 57

Church of Old Lyme...........*Hassam* 69

The Last Supper..............*Da Vinci* 77

St. Genevieve Watching over Paris.*De Chavannes* 89

The Fighting Téméraire........*Turner* 101

Victory of Samothrace......................113

INDEX OF ILLUSTRATIONS IN GREAT PICTURES AND THEIR STORIES

BOOK ONE—FIRST GRADE

(All in Color)   Page
1. Baby Stuart.................17
2. Nurse and Child............21
3. The Calmady Children......29
4. Madonna of the Chair......35
5. With Grandma.............42
6. Children of the Shell........51
7. Princess Margarita Theresia..58
8. Feeding her Birds..........66
9. Children of the Sea.........74
10. The Holy Night.............83

BOOK TWO—SECOND GRADE

(All in Color)   Page
1. A Holiday..................13
2. Mme. Lebrun and Her
   Daughter................21
3. Don Carlos on Horseback....28
4. The Boy With a Rabbit......37
5. The Storage Room..........45
6. The Pastry Eaters.........53
7. The Age of Innocence.......61
8. Home Work................69
9. Children of Charles I......77
10. Sistine Madonna...........84

BOOK THREE—THIRD GRADE

(All in Color)   Page
1. Miss Bowles...............13
2. Hearing...................20
3. Dancing in a Ring..........29
4. Angel With a Lute.........37
5. An Aristocrat.............45
6. Carnation, Lily, Lily, Rose...53
7. Return to the Fold.........61
8. Pilgrims Going to Church....69
9. Going to Church, Moravia....77
10. The Primitive Sculptor......85

BOOK FOUR—FOURTH GRADE

(All in Color)   Page
1. Aurora.....................13
2. The Horse Fair............25
3. Behind the Plow...........35
4. Venetian Waters...........47
5. The Sheepfold.............59
6. The Gleaners..............69
7. The Solemn Pledge.........81
8. Preparing for Church.......93
9. Going to Market..........103
10. The Blue Boy.............115

BOOK FIVE—FIFTH GRADE

(9 in Color—Statue in Black)   Page
1. Spring Dance...............13
2. After a Summer Shower......25
3. The Sewing School..........33
4. Russian Winter............41
5. Return of the Fishermen.....49
6. Song of the Lark...........61
7. Santa Fe Trail............72
8. Appeal to the Great Spirit....81
9. Lady With a Lute..........93
10. Galahad the Deliverer.....105

BOOK SIX—SIXTH GRADE

(9 in Color—Statue in Black)   Page
1. The Jester.................13
2. The Mill..................21
3. A Flower Girl of Holland....33
4. View of Ghent.............45
5. A Dutch Interior..........53
6. The Fog Warning..........65
7. Joan of Arc...............73
8. Joan of Arc...............85
9. Christ in the Temple.......93
10. The Angelus..............105

BOOK SEVEN—SEVENTH GRADE

(9 in Color—Statue in Black)   Page
1. Moonlight, Wood's Island
   Light....................13
2. Sir Galahad...............25
3. The Vigil.................37
4. Dance of the Nymphs.......45
5. Icebound..................57
6. The Concert...............65
7. King Cophetua and the
   Beggar Maid.............77
8. Frieze of the Prophets (Detail) 89
9. Bartolomeo Colleoni........101
10. Avenue of Trees..........109

BOOK EIGHT—EIGHTH GRADE

(9 in Color—Statue in Black   Page
1. George Washington.........13
2. On the Stairs.............25
3. Cotopaxi..................33
4. Syndics of the Cloth Guild....45
5. The Artist's Mother.......57
6. Church at Old Lyme........69
7. The Last Supper...........77
8. St. Genevieve.............89
9. The Fighting Temeraire.....101
10. Victory of Samothrace......113

BOOK NINE—FOR JR. AND SR. HIGH AND NORMAL SCHOOLS

     Page
1. James Whitcomb Riley.......10
2. The Mill Pond..............22
3. The Northeaster............30
4. The Whistling Boy..........42
5. Men of the Docks..........54

     Page
6. The Virgin..................66
7. King Lear..................78
8. Battersea Bridge...........90
9. The Apotheosis of Pittsburgh.102
10. Abraham Lincoln.......... 114

FOREWORD

Picture Study is rapidly becoming an important factor in our public school education. "Nearly every progressive city," says the Bureau of Education, Washington, D. C., "is making use of some form of picture study in the public school system."

The twentieth century has ushered in the reproduction of masterpieces in colors! To what heights of delight the children of the public schools may be carried by the famous pictures of the world in color!

It remains only for the elders to choose pictures adapted to the childish interests; pictures which will cultivate a taste for the best in art; pictures which through the impressionable early years will lead to a true understanding and appreciation of the world's masterpieces!

In preparing this series of readers it has been the aim of those selecting the pictures to consider always the child interest. The field of pictures is large. Not only have the "old masters" been drawn upon, but masters in modern art as well, including modern American artists. Thus constantly, through this series of pictures, the principles of beauty which made possible the "old masters" of yesterday are seen again in the art of today.

In the preparation of the text the child's interest and his ability to read are carefully considered. Real picture knowledge is conveyed in the child's own language.

In the primary grades the interest is largely in "what it is all about." Consequently the text aims to satisfy this curiosity, and at the same time lead to unconscious observation of those things which are most alive to the little child,—color, life, action.

The vocabulary for Books I, II, and III is based on "The Reading Vocabulary," * the Horn, Horn, and Packer List.

---

*See twenty-fourth Year Book, National Society for the Study of Education, Part I, 1925.

In the intermediate grades, a lively interest in the story is always uppermost. Gradually an appreciation of picture-pattern develops. Simple elements in picture making,—i.e. center of interest, repetition of line and color,— may be intelligently comprehended by children of the intermediate grades.

In the grammar grades great interest in the story continues, and with this interest there develops an appreciation of HOW the story is told,—the real ART of the picture. The pupil not only learns that the picture is a masterpiece, but WHY. He thus acquires standards for judging other pictures.

Each picture is followed by a short sketch of the artist, told in a key adapted to the age and interest of the pupil.

The questions which follow the text will assist in developing an intelligent appreciation of the picture.

The author is particularly indebted to Miss Jennie Long, recently Supervisor of Primary

Education, Peoria Public Schools, for valuable criticism of the primary text. Grateful acknowledgment is also made for the opportunity of practical work with a selected number of primary stories in the schools of Peoria.

The manuscripts of the intermediate and grammar grade books have been submitted to teachers of these grades, to whom the author is indebted for helpful practical suggestions.

The MUSICAL SELECTIONS for the pictures have been graciously contributed by Eva G. Kidder, Director of Music, Peoria Public Schools. The author believes this to be a very valuable feature of these books.

KATHERINE MORRIS LESTER.

ILLUSTRATED WITH REPRO-
DUCTIONS IN COLOR FROM
THE ORIGINAL MASTER-
PIECES, BY COURTESY OF
THE ART EXTENSION
SOCIETY OF NEW YORK.

GEORGE WASHINGTON
Metropolitan Museum, New York

ARTIST: Gilbert Stuart
SCHOOL: American
DATES: 1755-1828

GEORGE WASHINGTON

Gibbs-Channing Portrait

"Mr. Stuart,
    Chestnut St.
        Philadelphia.
"Dear Sir:
    I am under promise to Mrs. Bingham to sit for you tomorrow at 9 o'clock, and wishing to know if it be convenient to you that I should do so, and whether it be at your own house (as she talked of the State-house) I send this note to you to ask information.
    I am, Sir, your obt. servant,
                Geo. Washington.
Monday, 11th April, 1796."

From the dim past comes this note, signed by Washington himself, inquiring about his appointment with the famous artist, Gilbert Stuart. Over a century has gone. The portraits of Washington are priceless. Gilbert Stuart is the greatest portrait painter of early America.

It is said that Stuart painted as many as forty portraits of Washington, but only three from life.

The note quoted above and dated 1796 evidently arranged for a second or third sitting, for we know that Stuart's first portrait of Washington was painted in 1795.

For some reason Stuart was not pleased with this first painting. He is said to have destroyed it. Fortunately, however, three paintings were made in replica. Our famous Gibbs-Channing portrait is one of these.

A distinguishing characteristic of these first portraits by Stuart is that they show the right side of the face, while the later ones are taken from the left side.

In this famous painting Washington wears the conventional powdered hair, tied with a black ribbon. He wears the full neck cloth and ruffled shirt or jabot. This fits into the V-shaped opening of the black velvet coat. The head and shoulders are silhouetted against the curtained background. In the upper part of the painting the artist has kept the curtain dark, thus bringing out by contrast the fine line of the head and the freshness of the flesh tones. Toward the shoulders the tone of the curtain grows lighter, emphasizing again by contrast the dark form of the shoulder and coat. Beyond the lifted curtain one catches a glimpse of light cloud and sky, which repeat the lighter tones in the portrait. In thus arranging the "lights" and "darks" the artist gives his painting design form. Though all the details of lighting have been carefully thought out, it is the feeling for character in the head that distinguishes the Stuart portraits.

Here the head is firmly drawn and the color laid on in a broad simple way without attention to the details of shading. The coat, too, is a simple flat pattern of dark. Thus the artist has kept all parts of his picture subordinate to his main idea,—the head of Washington.

When once speaking of his portraits of Washington, the artist is quoted as saying: "I do not pretend to have painted Washington as the General of the Armies of Independence; I know him not as such. I have painted the President of the United States."

Though portraits, of a kind, have existed for a thousand years or more, it is only within the last five hundred years that portraits of real men and women, exactly as they appeared, have been painted. Even in these late portraits, artists differ in their ideas of just what a portrait should be. One prefers to paint every little detail, every little wrinkle, every eyelash, thinking that portraiture is an *exact* reproduction of the physical appearance. Another has a different idea. He gives scant attention, if any, to physical details, but seizes on the big characteristics,—the intellect, or some outstanding feature of personality. These he paints in a bold, simple way, aiming to interpret the real person behind the physical exterior.

This, undoubtedly, was Gilbert Stuart's way of working. Being once asked why he did not give more attention to the details of dress in his pictures, he replied: "I paint the works of God, and leave clothes to the tailor and the mantuamaker."

Stuart showed great preference for this portrait of Washington. For many years he kept it in his own possession. Finally, because of his friendship for Colonel George Gibbs, he disposed of it to him. It next passed to the sister of Colonel Gibbs, Mrs. William Ellery Channing; hence the name, — "Gibbs-Channing" portrait. This celebrated painting is now the valued possession of the Metropolitan Museum of New York City.

A second portrait, the last painted from life, and known as the "Athenæum" head now hangs in the Boston Museum of Fine Arts. This portrait was never completed for the artist hoped thus to keep it for himself.

THE ARTIST

Gilbert Stuart is America's most distinguished portrait painter of early days. Not only did he paint the portraits of presidents, generals, and conspicuous patriots on this side of the Atlantic, but in Europe the same honors came to him. In France, Louis XVI sat for his portrait; in London he painted the portraits of George III, the Prince of Wales, and other celebrities of the day.

Stuart was born in Rhode Island, December 3, 1755, of Scotch and Welsh parentage. At a very early age he began to show signs of great talent. One day, when only five years old, he overheard his mother and a neighbor discussing an absent acquaintance. He took a pencil, and much to the surprise of both, drew a likeness of the absent friend. When fifteen years of age his talent was so marked that it attracted wide attention. Among those who took particular interest in the boy was a wealthy Scotchman, who happened to be traveling in this country. He persuaded the parents to permit the youth to accompany him to Edinburgh.

In Scotland, Stuart applied himself diligently, spending two years in study at the University of Glasgow. Later, however, his benefactor died, and young Stuart, left penniless, was forced to return to America. He continued his studies, and made much progress. By 1775 he had again crossed the Atlantic and settled in London, where he studied with the well known American artist, Benjamin West. He forged rapidly ahead, and soon won fame. With fame came a distinguished patronage.

Stuart was living in England and at the very height of his success during our Revolutionary period. Later he was seized with a great ambition to paint the portrait of President Washington.   In 1792, in the midst of his great successes in London, he left England and returned to America.   He came for the sole purpose of painting the distinguished American.

No sooner had he reached America than word came from the Duke of Kent, father of Queen Victoria, requesting him to return to England for the purpose of painting his portrait. The Duke graciously offered to send a man-of-war to carry the young artist to England.   This was, indeed, a very distinguished honor.   Stuart, however, was so ardent an admirer of the American President that not even an invitation from the Queen's father could turn him back!

It was in 1794 that the painter took a residence in Philadelphia.   Some little time elapsed before he called upon the president.   One day, however, he set out, carrying with him a letter of introduction from the Hon. John Jay.   Not being able to see Washington, he left the letter with his card. Very promptly, to his surprise and pleasure, he received a cordial invitation to spend an evening with the President. Stuart relates that on this occasion he found Washington most courteous. His calm, dignified presence quite overawed him. Though accustomed to meet the most distinguished men of his day, he confesses that in the presence of Washington he lost, for a moment, his self-possession.*

It was doubtless on this occasion that arrangements were made for Washington to sit for his first portrait, which was painted in 1795.

It is said that these mornings in his studio were delightful. Washington was always accompanied by his two friends, General Henry Knox and Henry Lee. It was this same Lee who later, when delivering his eulogy on Washington, first coined the famous

*For interesting discussion of Washington's courtly manner from the Virginian point of view, see Life of Washington by General Bradley T. Johnson (pp. 18 and 19).

lines,—"First in war, first in peace, and first in the hearts of his countrymen."

In the studio they chatted together, relieving in a measure the tediousness of the long sittings. Stuart himself was a brilliant conversationalist. It is said that his manner and charm while working captivated his hearers. In fact this was a part of the painter's art. It brought to the surface feeling and expression which he seized upon in interpreting the character of his subject.

Though he painted the portraits of other presidents, it is portraits of Washington that are always associated with the name of Gilbert Stuart. A century has passed since the artist's death in 1828. During that time his genius has been increasingly honored and his fame more firmly established. In the perspective of a hundred years, Gilbert Stuart stands first among contemporary painters of our early national life.

STUDY FOR APPRECIATION

1. How many portraits of Washington did Stuart paint direct from life? What is characteristic of the first portraits? Of the later?
2. What is a portrait "in replica"?
3. Describe the dress of Washington, —his coat, his shirt, his hair.
4. Why has he kept the upper curtain dark? Why does it grow lighter toward the lower part?
5. Where has the artist placed his emphasis in this painting? How?
6. Give two ways in which an artist may paint a portrait. Which do you like best? Why?
7. Who is the painter of this portrait? How does he rank as an American artist?
8. Why is this portrait called the "Gibbs-Channing" portrait? Where does it hang today?

Related Music: AMERICA ....*Carey*

UPON THE STAIRS
Private Collection

ARTIST: Anders Zorn
SCHOOL: Swedish
DATES: 1860-1920

UPON THE STAIRS

A passing moment! An instantaneous impression! The sunlight falls full upon this angular stairway and the girl in rich, vibrant color descending.

No laborious painting this! No days and days of striving for effect. Here the artist, inspired by the beauty of the passing moment, records his impression easily and quickly.

The old stairway angles and turns. Up and up it goes. The angular composition and the strong diagonal lines give movement to the whole canvas.

How different the effect had the staircase been drawn in strong vertical and horizontal lines! Such a composition would have given repose. It would have lacked spontaneity. It would have lacked vigor. It would have lacked movement.

To the artist this scene was filled with the vigorous movement of light, and his choice of line in the angular staircase suggests this movement.

See the golden sunlight! It turns the staircase to brilliant yellow and tints of orange. It is reflected in a golden patch upon the side of the house. Its glowing light to right and left of the figure emphasizes and enriches the vibrant colors of the peasant dress. The brilliant red apron, the green jacket with patches of white, the great fur coat turned yellow-green, and the face, touched with sunlight, is a glowing center where the sun has concentrated its essence!

Notice the broad simple surface of the apron, jacket, and coat. Notice the simple planes of color in the staircase. This bold, direct way of painting gives vitality and spirit to the whole canvas. It is a distinguishing characteristic of this artist's style.

Above stands a second figure, subordinate, yet adding interest to the upper part of the picture. Notice how this figure bends, repeating the diagonal line of the staircase which forms the background. Notice how the arm falls in with the line of the balustrade upon which he leans. By posing his figure in this way the artist makes all the movement of the picture swing together. In this way he secures a rhythmic quality in his painting.

Notice again, he repeats the color also. The color of the girl's great coat is seen again, toned off, in the coat of the figure above. This carries the eye easily to the upper part of the canvas without detracting from the central figure. Thus, unconsciously, one sees all over the picture, as he should, and then quite as easily comes back to the sparkling light and color of the "center of interest."

"Vigorous," "vital," "bold," "spontaneous," are words invariably applied to the works of this distinguished artist. In this painting—"Upon the Stairs" —these characteristic qualities give to the picture spirit and charm.

THE ARTIST

Anders Zorn is Sweden's greatest painter. It was in 1860, in the little village of Mora, that Zorn was born. This section of Sweden is a lonely region of timber land dotted with lakes and rivers. Though far removed from the large centers, it made its impression on the young lad, for in after years when fame had come to him, he found his greatest joy in living and painting among his own people in the little village of Mora.

When a lad of fifteen Anders Zorn began to show remarkable talent. His great enthusiasm for carving led his parents to believe that he was destined to be a sculptor. A number of his father's friends collected a small sum of money, sufficient to send him to the Art Academy of Stockholm.

Finding later that the possibility of further study depended on his own efforts, he set to work making pencil portraits. These he sold for a modest sum. He kept at this for some time, but at the end of two years was forced to return home penniless.

Years after he laughingly told how his mother reproached him, saying: "If you had done as I wished and gone to learn to be a tailor, you would be getting four kronen a week now."

By and by, in 1882, after sufficient money had been earned and saved, he started for England. Arriving there, he boldly set up a studio. Fortunately attention turned his way. Soon he was engaged to paint the portraits of the various members of the Swedish legation. From this time on his star was in the ascendent. He became famous not only for his paintings, but for his etchings as well.

Zorn was always eager to learn. After success came to him, he studied in the great museums of France, Italy, and Spain. He traveled constantly for a number of years, frequently visiting America. During these visits, many of them prolonged, he painted the portraits of several distinguished Americans.

Though he won international fame, he chose as his home the little village of Mora, his birthplace. He preferred to dwell there among his own people, delighting in the picturesque country and the colorful costumes of the peasantry. Here Zorn lived,—"the uncrowned king," — bestowing his kindnesses upon the peasants of Mora. They in turn loved and honored their kinsman.

It is said that on public occasions or holidays of any kind, the festivities never began until the beloved figure of Zorn appeared. Further, it is due to his influence that the peasants still retain their picturesque dress.

Though many paintings of this famous artist hang in America, it is the art collections of his native land that claim the greater number of his works.

STUDY FOR APPRECIATION

1. When is a painter said to be an "Impressionist"?
2. Why did this subject appeal to the artist?
3. What gives color to the painting?
   From what direction comes the light?
   How do you know?
4. What gives movement to the painting?
   What is the most forceful line?
5. How is the eye led over the picture?
6. How has the artist made the figure of the girl important?
   Do the shadows help? How?
7. Describe the colors and values in the girl's dress.
   Are any colors repeated? Where?
   Does this add to the picture? How?
8. Who is the artist?
   What is his nationality?
   What are the outstanding characteristics of his work?

Related Music: SHADOW DANCE......
MacDowell

COTOPAXI, ECUADOR
New York Public Library

ARTIST: Frederick E. Church
SCHOOL: American
DATES: 1826-1900

COTOPAXI

"The most beautiful and most terrible of American volcanoes" is Cotopaxi. This remarkable volcano of South America rises from the eastern chain of the Andes, rearing its summit 18,858 feet above sea level.

For many years a column of smoke poured constantly from the crater. Occasionally terrific explosions were heard. These were accompanied by great volumes of smoke and ashes that filled the air.

Cotopaxi has had several notable eruptions. In April, 1768, the most terrible of all took place. For hours smoke and ashes poured forth from the crater, until the country round about became so dark that the people were forced to grope their way about with lanterns.

In this famous painting the artist has pictured the very top of the mountain chain. In the distance, some fifty miles away, one sees the dim outlines of the tall gray cone. Above it the dense black vapor is constantly rising. After it has risen several thousand feet, the wind carries it off in a diagonal direction where it hangs low and heavy along the horizon.

The sun is rising. Its dazzling light cannot pierce the dense volume of smoke. It shines as through a smoked glass, lighting up the scene with a low, lurid glow.

Eighteen thousand feet above sea level! Fifty miles of mountain! Cotopaxi in continuous eruption. Such is the scene painted by the American artist, Frederick E. Church. Unlike many landscape painters, this artist had an eye only for the grand, sublime and spectacular aspects of nature. His pictures cover large areas, and are generally composed in large simple masses. Here the expanse of sky is broken by the great smoke cloud. Variety is given the foreground by the volcanic lake and the cascades formed by the overflow of water.

The volcanic lake and the cascades are frequently seen in the Andes. The lakes are often formed during an eruption, when chasms become filled with water. When filled to overflowing the water drops over the edge of the rocks, forming sparkling cascades as it pours down the steep sides of the mountains.

See the dull reflection of the sun as it crosses the lake! This is not brilliant, dazzling sunlight such as one may expect to see from the summit of a lofty mountain. It is a dimly opaque glow, making its way through the overhanging vapor.

It is said that the atmospheric effect of smoke has never been painted more accurately than in this picture. The pale glow of the sun reaches even down to the foreground of the picture, where it touches the ridges of sandstone rock with its light.

Someone has said that this is "one of the truest and most exquisite effects of light ever produced."

The porous, reddish limestone rocks of the foreground, columnar in form, are characteristic of this chain of the Andes. A rough, green vegetation creeps over the arid soil. It grows more abundant as it nears the foreground of the picture, where a few trees break the lonely stretch of mountain top.

See how the artist leads into his picture! The eye follows along the irregular rock edge of the cascade; on to the lake with its low ominous light; then, in an instant, the dark mass of belching smoke from the crater centers our attention. This is Cotopaxi, the terrible!

It is a realistic picture of a region few are privileged to see, the mountain top of the Andes. The peculiarities of sky and rock, of color and light, under the conditions of volcanic eruption, are said to be faithfully pictured by the artist. He belongs to a group of early American painters who were the pioneers of landscape art in this country. Enthusiastic lovers of nature, they were possessed by the one ambition, to set her beauties and wonders accurately upon canvas for all the world to see!

THE ARTIST

It is not surprising that the Rip Van Winkle country of the Catskills was the inspiration of the early landscape painters of America. Lofty mountains, range upon range, wooded slopes, glittering cascades, gorges, rocks and ledges,—these were the picturesque haunts of our early landscape artists. This group of painters has passed into history as, "The Hudson River School." Among the most prominent is Frederick E. Church.

Though born in Hartford, Connecticut, in 1826, Church began his studies in the Catskills. When a mere youth he showed great talent for drawing. Later, when he decided to become an artist, his parents made arrangements for him to study with one of the artists then living in the Catskills. There he lived and worked under the direction of his new teacher. There he studied the grand aspects of nature just as she appeared. He watched the changes of sky, clouds, trees, the form of the mountains, the rising and setting of the sun.

Later he painted his pictures, giving the people of that early day an idea of the great and beautiful world in which they lived. His pictures were received with enthusiasm. People paid fabulous prices for his canvases.

In this early day it was considered necessary that all artists go to Europe to study, and to gather new ideas of light effects and color. Church, however, did not go to Europe for study.

Instead, he traveled to distant countries, using his great gift of "intelligent seeing" to gather the subjects for his pictures.

In South America the volcanic region about Quito absorbed him. The lofty mountains, the tropical skies and atmosphere, the volcanic chain of the Andes, were a profound inspiration to him. The artist's travels were fraught with hardship and peril, but his great desire to secure new themes for his brush led him to brave any danger. He climbed dizzy heights, canoed through unexplored streams, forced his way through tropical forests, to find just the sublime aspects of nature that he wanted.

On one occasion, after days of heat and sea-sickness, he with his companion and guides left their boats at the mouth of the Magdalena river, took their mules, and started through a dense forest, thick with an undergrowth of tropical vegetation. By accident he and his companion became separated from the guides. Soon night came on. They completely lost their way. Sinking knee-deep into a morass here and there, becoming entangled in trailing vines, the only escape seemed to be in the tall trees. He and his companion climbed to the top of a tree. There they shouted for help. There was no response, save the hooting of owls and the roars of wild animals. By morning the mules had disappeared. Though weary almost to the point of exhaustion, they made another desperate effort to find the track to the guides. Soon their efforts were crowned with success. Trials and fatigue were forgotten as they joyfully continued their journey.

It was this visit to South America that inspired his two famous pictures —"Cotopaxi," and "The Heart of the Andes."

From the heart of the tropics, Church traveled to the cold of the polar regions. Everywhere, at this period, people were interested in arctic discovery. This was a new field that made its appeal to the artist. He decided to study the cold north. Accordingly he went to the west coast of Labrador, where icebergs could be seen to the best advantage. Here he lived with the fishermen and the missionaries. After studying the sky and light effects for some time, he took a boat and set out to study icebergs. Icebergs are among the most difficult objects of nature to paint. Many were the trials and vexations of the expedition, sweetened by a saving sense of humor, and offset by the joy of success.

As a result of this visit, "The Icebergs" was exhibited in London in 1863. It was enthusiastically received as a "noble example of the landscape-painter's art," and especially praised for its rendering of the "grand, beautiful, and unfamiliar aspects of nature."

Among the majestic scenes of American landscape, Niagara Falls is the most famous. True to his custom, Church journeyed to the Falls, and there studied their every feature—the vast rush of water, the curling mist, the unusual atmospheric effects. These he transferred to a canvas seven feet long by three feet high. Immediately it was received as an "exact and superb reproduction of this wonder of our western world." This painting has become generally familiar through many chromo-lithographic copies.

Always it is the superb, the sublime, that which is in the "grand style," this painter chooses for his subjects. In the group of the Hudson River School Frederick E. Church stands foremost as expressing the aims and ideals of this particular period. The art of today looks back to this school of yesterday as having laid the foundation for a national landscape art in the new America.

STUDY FOR APPRECIATION

1. What region of America first inspired our early landscape painters? Under what name was this group of painters known?
2. Who was foremost in this group?
3. What was the type of landscape painted at this period? How does it differ from the landscape of today?
4. Where is the scene of this painting? Name the large areas in the picture.
5. How does the artist lead into the picture? Where is the eye carried? Why?
6. How is the "center of interest" made important?
7. Describe the sun. What is the dominant color of the picture? What does this color suggest?
8. Name one other painting of this artist.

Related Music: RIDE OF VALKYRIES..
................*Wagner*

43

SYNDICS OF THE CLOTH GUILD
Rijksmuseum, Amsterdam

ARTIST: Rembrandt van Rijn
SCHOOL: Dutch
DATES: 1606=1669

SYNDICS OF THE CLOTH GUILD

Five hundred years ago the great trade fraternities and trade guilds of Europe were flourishing. History tells us that even much earlier workers were uniting for mutual aid and protection. All who made shoes were banded in the "Guild of Shoemakers"; those who made armour in the "Guild of Armourers"; those who were weavers in the "Guild of Weavers." So it was with every trade and craft of consequence. Each had its own house or gathering place. These were called "Guild Houses."

In Holland and Belgium the guilds were of great importance. The king usually appointed the general officers. The members themselves, however, chose their directors or syndics, as they were called.

It was quite the fashion in this day for groups, from the various guilds, to have their portraits painted.

This was, indeed, the day of the group portrait! Many were the orders that came to the artists for such paintings. Usually each man paid his share for his place upon the canvas. He expected an excellent likeness. Great was the dissatisfaction if one of the group received more light or better color than another!

"Syndics of the Cloth Guild" is such a painting. The directors of the cloth guild commissioned the great Dutch artist, Rembrandt van Rijn, to paint their portraits. Probably they planned to hang the painting, when completed, in the great Guild Hall. There they would be constantly in attendance upon the meetings of the guild members.

At any rate, Rembrandt had a puzzling problem. Here were five men. They were all dressed alike, black coats, white collars, and high steeple hats.

How could an artist make a worthy picture of so monotonous a group! But

Rembrandt was a man of genius. He chose for his setting one end of the guild hall. Here stood the directors' table. It was a long heavy table, and stood upon a dais or raised platform at the end of the room. We know the table was upon a raised platform because the perspective lines show it. Over the table he threw a woven cloth.

Having selected the setting for his picture, he must next arrange the group. Here is where he shows himself the artist. How stupid had the five men been sitting in an even row! Never could Rembrandt make so dull an arrangement!

As he planned his picture he doubtless thought to himself: "I shall put these directors in meeting. I shall place them around their directors' table. The workers shall sit in the hall below. By and by, someone will rise to speak. Immediately, the eyes of all the directors shall be fixed upon the speaker."

So thinking, he arranged his men about the table. Just as he had surmised, someone has risen to speak! The directors' eyes are full upon him.

See the interested expression of the faces! One dignified syndic rises and looks over the audience. He hopes to obtain a better view of the speaker. Just as the artist planned, this breaks the even row of heads!

Five black coats, five white collars, five tall hats, all alike! Five faces, each one different! Each a study in itself! The central figure is presiding, with his open book before him. His attention is directed toward the speaker. His friend at the right smiles faintly. He is much amused. At the far right the treasurer, who holds the money bag, is greatly surprised. How dignified is the director at the far left! He sits unruffled, and looks out over the assembly.

Watch the expression of these five faces. Each is different. Each expresses marked individuality. Someone has said that Rembrandt painted these heads "so true to life that in the course of the years they have become like old friends; yes, old friends, though they lived hundreds of years before we were dreamed of."

See the marvelous intelligence in the faces! See the life and understanding in the eyes!

The rich dark tone of the table cloth breaks into a glowing red where the light strikes it. This brilliant touch serves to give depth to the painting. It is repeated in the flesh tints, and again, toned off, in the warm hue of the wainscoting. Behind the directors stands the serving man. The painter is not so interested, perhaps, in his portrait. The figure, however, is an artistic means of giving variety and color to the back wall.

The arrangement of the group was indeed a happy one. The rich velvety blacks and the white collars against the dark brown of the wainscoting emphasize the flesh tones, and the interesting expression of the faces. No group could be arranged in a more simple way, and no portraits could be better!

This has been pronounced the greatest of Rembrandt's paintings, perfect in every particular,—drawing, color, expression, and composition.

THE ARTIST

Rembrandt van Rijn is the greatest name in Dutch painting. Strange as it may seem, it is only within recent years that the world has awakened to his unequaled genius. Holland now proudly points to him as one of her own sons.

The artist of the sixteenth and seventeenth centuries was not heralded by newspapers, magazines, and exhibits, as he is in the twentieth century. Unless an artist happened to gain the attention of a king or some noble of distinction, his life and talent often remained obscure. Rembrandt was not favored by kings and courts; consequently the records of his life are scanty.

Though the exact year of his birth is unknown, it is believed to have been between 1602 and 1607. The quaint little town of Leyden claims the honor of being his birthplace. It was here in the fascinating surroundings of a Dutch town that the boy spent his early years. In Leyden he received his first schooling. He proved to be far more rapid with the pencil than in the common branches of study. It is said that his teacher was greatly annoyed because the boy would sit and look out of the window, his mind in dreamland, rather than attend to his lessons. One day the master's patience reached its limit, and he tried flogging. Next morning he found a picture of himself, and not a flattering likeness either, drawn upon the blackboard.

He sent for the father. The father came. The schoolmaster, pointing to the likeness upon the board, said: "See what your son has done! He will do nothing but draw pictures." The father looked hard and long at the picture. Then he replied, calmly, "But it is a good likeness." Then he took the boy home to his mother.

The mother was a wise little woman. "If he really wishes only to draw pictures," said she, "we must let him draw pictures." Forthwith, through his mother's influence, he was sent to one of the best drawing masters. Here he learned many things.

He learned how to spread a thin layer of wax on a brass plate, to draw a picture on the wax, and then to pour acid over the plate. The acid ate into the brass on the sketched lines. This made a plate from which pictures could be rapidly printed. This manner of working, which was a delight to Rembrandt, is known as "etching." He etched many of the pictures which he made while studying with this master.

Today his etchings, something like six hundred in number, are well known. He is distinguished as an etcher of rare ability, as well as one of the great world painters.

After some years at Leyden, the father took his little family to Amsterdam, where the great part of Rembrandt's life was spent. Many were the anxieties and perplexities of the artist's life. People did not understand his art. They censured him for not following in the footsteps of the great masters of the past. They condemned him for wasting his time. They snarled at him for being different. But Rembrandt kept right on.

The subject of light and shade interested him most. Through his understanding of light, all his shadows become deep and velvety. Then, from these depths, he permits only certain parts of his picture to come out into full light. These are the most important parts, usually the faces. In this way he concentrated attention upon the essential part of the picture. Notice that in his painting, "Syndics of the Cloth Guild," it is the faces that reflect the full light coming in at the window. He understood a painting to be a scheme of tone, color, and mass, rather than line.

Rembrandt was a popular painter, but his full powers were not understood. He passed away with the world blind to his genius.

Today people travel across continents to see his pictures. One small painting would bring a fortune,—if it could be bought. The old house in Amsterdam, where he lived, is prized. Everything that had to do with this painter is worth more than its weight in gold. How the world has changed in five hundred years!

STUDY FOR APPRECIATION

1. What were the guilds?
   Why were they organized?
2. Who are these men?
   In what country did they live?
   When?
3. What was the fashionable type of portraiture in that day?
4. What was the artist's problem in this painting?
   How did the artist give variety to the group?
5. From what direction comes the light?
   What parts of the picture are lighted?
6. Describe the expression of the faces.
   Which of the group would you like best to know? Why?
7. Name the colors and values in the table cover and wall.
8. Who is the artist?
   Where did he live? When?
   Describe his way of painting.

Related Music: LARGHETTO—Second
Symphony .....*Beethoven*

AN ARRANGEMENT IN GRAY AND BLACK
Louvre, Paris

ARTIST: James McNeil Whistler
SCHOOL: American
DATES: 1834-1903

AN ARRANGEMENT IN GRAY AND BLACK

The Artist's Mother

One of the most famous pictures painted by an American artist and owned by a foreign government is this portrait, "The Artist's Mother," by James McNeil Whistler. The painting was purchased by the French government in 1891. It is only within recent years that the picture has been given the name, "The Artist's Mother," for Whistler himself called it, "An Arrangement in Gray and Black."

This seems a strange name for a picture. Whistler, however, had ideas of his own about painting. These ideas were very new, and very different from those of other artists. He declared that it is never the person, object, or thing painted that is of consequence, but always the *way it is painted*. He continually emphasized what to him seemed so apparent—as "music is the poetry of sound," so "painting is the poetry of sight." In other words his idea was to arrange and combine color into beautiful harmonies, harmonies as pleasing to the eye as is music to the ear. True, the subject of the picture is often a portrait, a bit of landscape or an interior; but this is only a means for a beautiful arrangement of color.

To make still more clear his meaning about color and color harmonies, he gave his pictures such names as,— "Study in Rose and Brown", "Harmony in Gray and Gold," "Symphony in White," "Nocturne in Blue and Silver"; always, you see, emphasizing the color, color harmony, and color arrangement.

In this "Arrangement of Gray and Black" one fairly sees the artist set his color-pattern to music. See the beautiful spacing of the canvas, wall, floor, curtain! So pleasing is the relation between wall and floor that neither could be changed. The gray-green curtain breaks the wall space. This leaves a softly lighted area for the figure. The mother takes her place. Soon the framed print suggests itself as a note of interest in the background space. Notice where it is placed! Could it be moved to the right? Could it be moved to the left? Could it be raised? Could it be lowered? The adding of a portion of a print to the right carries the interest out to the far edge of the canvas. The pattern is complete! The "arrangement" of space is perfect! Whistler called the picture an "arrangement" because it is fine in its related spaces, its pattern or composition. He also spoke of its harmonious color, calling it "an accord of color masses." Color makes the symphony complete!

Black, white, and grays! Seeing the picture at a distance, its surface melts into tones of gray,—the light warm gray wall, the medium gray floor, the still darker gray of the curtain. The black mass of the figure is framed against the warm gray wall. Only the head and hands attract, accented as they are by the notes of soft white lace. The white lawn and lace trimmed cap with its flowing ties, so delicately painted, add quiet charm to the gentle face. The lace cuffs and the dainty white kerchief carry the eye down to the hands. Then back again it passes to the head. It is always about the head, then the hand, and back again to the head, that the eye travels. Even though we go wandering off to the framed print, back again we come to the beautiful face and hands of the mother.

What a gentle lady she is! How the flesh tones sing out against the warm gray wall! The arms are limp. The hands lie in the lap. She sits in quiet reverie. How fitting the subdued tones to the subject of the painting!

Thus the artist planned his picture. To him it was an arrangement of picture—space and color harmony; so he called it "An Arrangement in Gray and Black."

When it was discovered that the painting was a portrait of the artist's mother, people began to call it "Mother of the Artist," and "The Artist's Mother." Whistler, however, felt that people should not be interested in it simply because it was a painting of his mother. Said he: "To me it is interesting as a picture of my mother; but what can or ought the public to care about the identity of the portrait." He felt that people should be interested in it for a far more important reason,—because it was a work of art, an artistic arrangement of picture-space and color harmony.

This portrait was painted when Whistler was at the very height of his power. Though not so regarded at the time, today it is acknowledged by art critics as among the masterpieces of the world.

THE ARTIST

Today all the world honors the name of James McNeil Whistler. Fifty years ago the same artist was criticized and ridiculed by an unappreciative public. How strange the changes wrought by time!

James McNeil Whistler was born in Lowell, Massachusetts, in 1834. Though he spent most of his life in foreign countries, America claims him as among her most distinguished artists. Whistler's father came of a line of soldiers. He was a graduate of West Point, and known as Major George Washington Whistler of the United States Army. At West Point he had won distinction as an engineer, and his reputation was such that he was commissioned to build important railroads in this country.

Naturally Whistler's mother was eager for her son to follow in the footsteps of his father, and enter the West

Point Academy. At an early age, however, Whistler developed so great a taste for drawing that a military career seemed unlikely.

When the boy was about eight years old Major Whistler was called to Russia by Czar Nicholas, to superintend the building of the railroad between Moscow and St. Petersburg. Going to Russia, he took the youthful James with him. Here in the Russian capital the growing boy spent seven years.

Returning to America, the plan of a military career for the young man was revived. In the end his mother's wish prevailed and he was sent to West Point. Here he made little advance in his studies, and at the end of the third year was dismissed. Though his grades in his major studies were not up to standard, he stood at the head of his class in drawing. His drawing of maps, in particular, was highly praised by his teachers.

Many are the stories told of his indifference to the studies at West Point. During an examination, young Whistler was asked to give the date of the battle of Buena Vista. He was unable to answer. "What," stormed the instructor, "do you not know the date of the battle of Buena Vista? Suppose you were in company at dinner, and you, a West Point man, should be asked about the Mexican War and the date of the battle,—what would you do?"

"Do, sir," replied Whistler, "I should refuse to associate with people who talked of wars and battles at dinner."

Such was the independence of Whistler in all his thinking. Later in his art this same independence of thought shocked the public into amazed and curious attention.

It was after his dismissal at West Point that his art career began in earnest. Going to Paris, he gave himself to his studies. He was a diligent student, a vigorous worker, and soon attracted public interest.

His art was different from that to which people had long been accustomed. They did not understand it. When he talked of painting in relation to music, and called his canvases "symphonies," "nocturnes," and "arrangements," they were first amused, then indignant. Many were the attacks made upon him.

Equally spirited was the artist's defense of his work. Whistler was brilliant in conversation and repartee, and his caustic replies to his critics brought him more and more into the public eye. In the end he became as well known for his wit as for his pictures.

Friends who knew him intimately say that the artist was possessed of two personalities. Out upon the public promenade he was one; working in his studio he was another.

He seldom appeared upon the streets in any other role than that of the man of fashion, the dandy. He was "a sprightly little man," always wearing the latest in linen and broadcloth. He took great pride in his small feet and very slender waist. He wore yellow gloves and carried a long slender cane, two-thirds his own height. This he invariably held at a very graceful angle. A slight "imperial" and waxed mustache added to his very dapper appearance, and a monocle was the finishing touch.

But in the studio how different! Here he was the tireless worker, the sincere student. Old clothes, heavy iron spectacles, wrapped about with cloth that they might rest more comfortably on his nose, and a generally unkempt appearance — this was the real Whistler. Here he was persevering to the utmost. He counted labor as nothing when striving to secure an exact tone or color. He was an artist to the very tips of his fingers.

Though in his own day he was regarded as fantastic and his ideas of artistic expression absurd, he has be-

come a recognized genius in the field
of American painting.

STUDY FOR APPRECIATION

1. Why is this painting called an
   "arrangement"?
   Point out the fine space rela-
   tions in the canvas.

2. What is meant by "an accord of
   color masses"?
   Name the color masses.
   Does the color bear any relation
   to the subject? What?

3. How many values do you find in
   the picture? What are they?

4. Where is the "center of interest"?
   How is it emphasized?

5. Who is the artist?

6. What was his theory about the art
   of picture-making?

Related Music: MOTHER OF MINE.. *Tours*
                 TRAUMEREI ... *Schumann*

CHURCH AT OLD LYME
Albright Gallery, New York

ARTIST: Childe Hassam
SCHOOL: American
DATES: 1859-1935

THE CHURCH OF OLD LYME

Down in New England, near the mouth of the Connecticut River, is the quaint town of Old Lyme. This region is typical New England country. Here stands a typical New England church, the church of Old Lyme.

It rises a mass of plain whiteness against the turquoise blue of the sky. Its four stately Ionic columns give a classic dignity to the entrance. Above towers the belfry.

See the brilliant New England sunshine! It sifts through the interlacing boughs. It plays over the church. It plays over the lawn, the walls, the trees. It dapples the whole scene! It brings to life the reds and greens of late autumn!

The old church is set in a frame of elms. They march back in regular line at the left. To the right the shadows on the white wall and the glimpse of foliage above suggest the tall trees that border the walk on this side.

See the lace-like pattern made by the long curving branches! See the powerful elm at the right!

No doubt it has seen many autumns such as this. See its sturdy trunk, ashen gray in the sunlight! See the vigor in its long branches!

Oh, yes, the artist knew trees. He knew their growth, their character. He knew their foliage, and the effect of glinting sunlight upon it.

The green firs at each side of the porch make a dark accent, framing in the beautiful classic entrance. Thus, you see the artist first frames in, with the tall elms, the larger setting; next, he places the smaller, darker accents, as a second note. These frame in the most important part of the picture, the classic columns and the arched doorway. This gives design form to the picture-pattern. This is the *art* of the picture.

See how the sun glints across the

lawn! Light green, dark green, and here and there patches of red!

All the rich red of autumn, however, has fallen this side of the little white posts. It is not so much the leaves, you see, but the light upon them that the artist paints.

To paint the effect of sunlight this artist often works with little spots of pure color, placing them side by side. This produces a very different effect from that of the earlier painters, who mixed their colors. It produces a vibrating light. It makes a picture of the atmosphere as it plays upon the landscape.

See the long lines of shadow across the lawn! They lead right up to the steps, then up to the door of the church. Below, the white church is patterned with the pale blue shadows that mark it. Above, the belfry is bathed in a warm yellow light.

See how the beautiful arch of the door is repeated again and again in the windows above, and then in the arching boughs of the elms! One after another, to right and to left, they bend and meet in archlike form above.

Indeed this repetition gives a beautiful rhythmic quality to the setting. It helps to make the design-pattern for his composition.

The artist was not unmindful of this repetition of line in his picture. He saw it again in the graceful height of the Ionic columns repeated in the tall trunks of the elms. He saw it still again in the little white posts that border the walk.

Light and air play over the entire canvas. It draws the reds, greens, blue, and white into one harmonious key, until the whole picture sings together in perfect tune.

This painting now hangs in the beautiful Albright gallery, in Buffalo, New York. Here one may study first hand the work of this gifted American painter, Childe Hassam.

THE ARTIST

Among the most distinguished American artists of today is Childe Hassam, the painter of sparkling light and color.

Mr. Hassam represents the modern style in painting. While the old masters mixed their colors to produce the subtle tones of light and shade, the modern painter often uses pure color. He places one spot or dot of pure color against another. This produces the effect of vibrating light. It gives sparkle and spirit to a picture.

Then, too, while the old masters confined themselves to religious subjects, the modern painter finds the world about him of absorbing interest. He sees the green fields, the flowers, the sea. He finds a new beauty in the busy streets of a great city; in the irregular outlines of distant skyscrapers, or the indistinct life of a busy wharf.

This love of the real world has produced the modern landscape painter. Among these modern painters Childe Hassam is a distinguished leader.

This painter of light and life was born in Boston in 1859. He grew up in the artistic atmosphere of that beauty-loving city. He was educated in the Boston Public Schools.

Later he went to Paris for study. His great ability, however, was largely self-developed. Childe Hassam knew what he wanted to do, and he went forth to do it.

He painted in the great out-of-doors. He painted exactly what he saw. He was thoroughly individual, painting only his own impression of a scene. For this reason he is known as an "impressionist" painter. He is one of the most successful of American painters in the use of pure pigment, "spotted in."

This manner of painting is expressive not so much of the material landscape as it is of the light and atmosphere that envelop it.

STUDY FOR APPRECIATION

1. What is an "impressionist" painter?
2. Where is the church of Old Lyme?
   To what period of American life
   does it belong?
3. Why is the entrance porch termed
   "classical"?
4. How is the picture framed in?
   How is the "center of interest"
   emphasized?
5. Where is the sun?
   What is the effect on the church?
   The belfry? Trees? Lawn?
   What unifies the various colors?
6. What gives the picture design-form?
   Point out the repetition of curves.
   Point out the repetition of vertical
   accents.
   Does this add to the picture value?
   How?
7. Who is the artist?
   What is his style in painting?

Related Music: O WORSHIP THE KING
.... *Haydn*
LARGO ....*Handel*

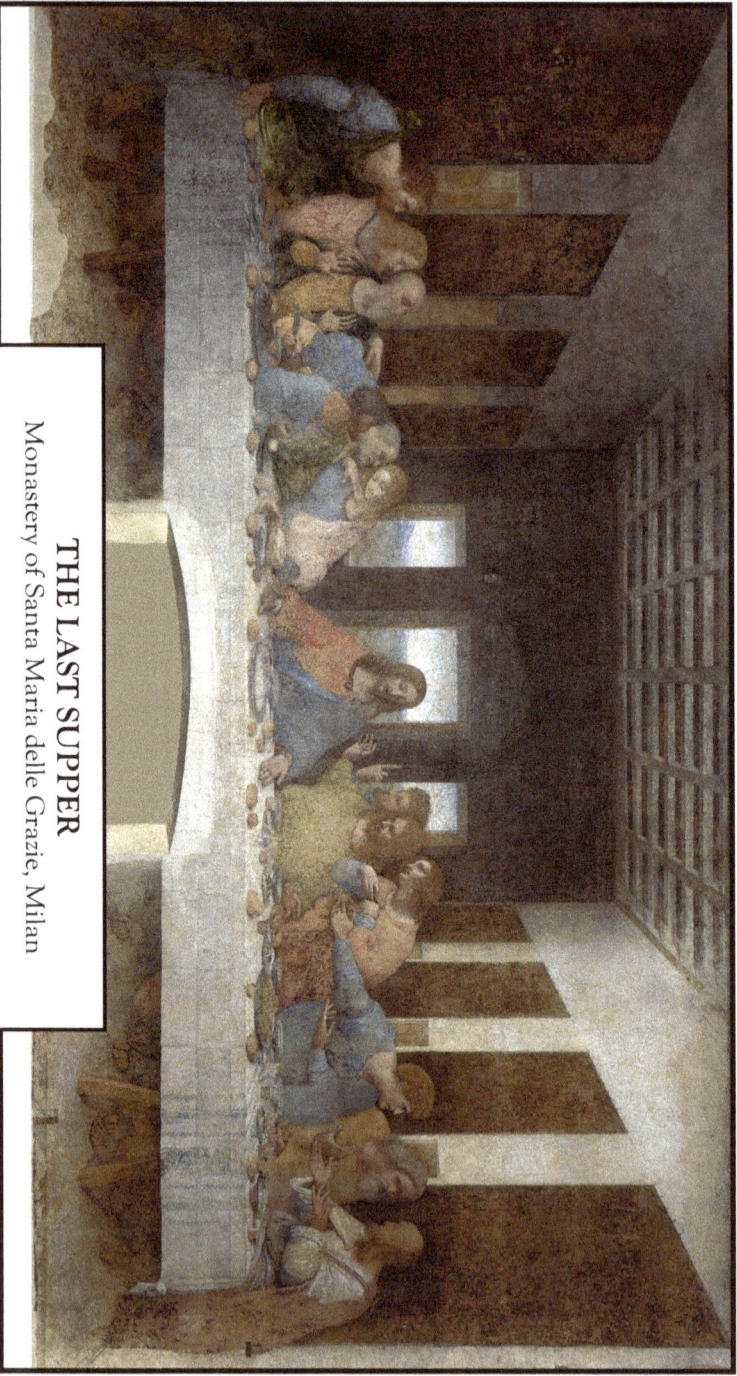

THE LAST SUPPER

Monastery of Santa Maria delle Grazie, Milan

ARTIST: Leonardo da Vinci
SCHOOL: Italian
DATES: 1452-1519

THE LAST SUPPER

Among the great fresco paintings of the world, "The Last Supper," by Leonardo da Vinci, has held a conspicuous place for the past four hundred years. Though mutilated, restored, and mutilated again, it still remains among the greatest of Italian wall-paintings.

This famous fresco was painted directly upon the wall of the old monastery of Santa Marie delle Grazie in Milan. The date according to the monastery records is 1497. This, you see, makes the fresco over four hundred years old. We are not surprised that it has "flaked off" during the passage of the years. We are told that the artist, instead of following the established rule for fresco, mixed his color with oil instead of water, to secure more brilliant hues. He little thought at the time that the world, four hundred years later, would regret his choice.

Though today this room in the old monastery is a shrine constantly visited by artists and travelers alike, it has not always been so highly esteemed. History tells us that Napoleon, in one of his Italian campaigns, quartered his horses in this room. His men were so little impressed by the painting that they used it as a target for missiles. Later a door was cut through the wall, defacing the lower center. Today the general design of the great picture is about all that remains of the original. Even in this state, however, it is recognized as one of the masterpieces of the world.

About four hundred years ago Italy awakened to a new artistic life. The patrons of art in that distant day were largely churchmen. For the great mass of the people, pictures were the most effective means of religious instruction. The artist told the story of the saints and martyrs in the language of picture, the language of design and color. All the people went to the churches. They studied the pictures. Through pictures they learned more of the saints, more of the holy men of the past, more of religion.

Not only the walls of the churches of this day, but the walls of monasteries as well, and other buildings associated with the life of the church, were decorated with subjects chosen from the Scriptures. The Last Supper was a favorite theme. It was considered especially appropriate for the dining-hall of a monastery. It was here that the monks gathered regularly. It was here, each day as they sat at meat, that the impressive lesson of the picture was imprinted upon their minds and hearts.

Though the most brilliant painters of Italy were inspired by the same subject, not one designed his picture as did Leonardo da Vinci. It is the beauty of design that makes this fresco, though sadly mutilated, a masterpiece.

The idea of seating the disciples at a long table grew, no doubt, out of a custom of the monks. It was their habit to file into the dining-hall three times each day, and seat themselves at the long tables. They doubtless made a picture similar to that of the decoration.

"And when even was come, he sat down with the twelve."

Jesus and his disciples had journeyed to the Holy City, Jerusalem. It was a day of celebration, commemorating the deliverance of the children of Israel from Egyptian bondage. They sat in an upper room having their evening meal together.

The artist pictures the large upper room in perfect perspective. See how the long lines of the ceiling and the vanishing lines of the side walls carry back, back, through the open window to the far Judean hills. This gives plenty of room for the long table and thirteen figures, each larger than life.

Jesus sits in the midst of his disciples. Six are arranged at the right, six at the left. They are conversing. Gradually the scene grows quiet. They hear strange words. The Master is speaking: "Verily, I say unto you, that one of you shall betray me."

The little company is shocked, horrified! They become excited and anxious. One by one they eagerly question: "Is it I? Is it I?"

We see the anxious group. We see the stricken faces. We see all questioning but Judas. He draws back. He holds in his hand the money bag. He sits third to the master's right.

See the arrangement of the group! The artist gave much thought to this. As the words, "One of you shall betray me," were spoken, the little company, in the excitement of the moment, breaks up into groups of three. To the master's right, John, the beloved disciple, is overcome by the words he hears; Peter, the impetuous one, leans over questioning; Judas draws back. These three form a close compact group. Next, James, the younger, Bartholomew, the scholar, and Andrew stand together, eagerly hanging upon the words of the teacher.

To the left, James the elder throws out his hands, recoiling from the thought of betrayal. Thomas raises his finger, as he asks excitedly, "Lord, is it I?"

Philip is deeply moved; he raises both hands to his breast as he questions, "Is it I?" In the last group, Matthew, with outstretched arms, turns and vehemently addresses the excited Thaddeus and Simon.

Thirteen men sit within the room. They are all forceful men. All, but one, are agitated and bewildered. We see the consternation and perplexity written in their features. Then we pass to the central figure, so calm and composed. The contrast is marked.

A true picture gives but one impression. So here the artist planned his picture in the form of one design. Though there are many figures, they are so arranged that they unite in one pattern, with the principal lines leading to the "center of interest."

Continue the perspective lines of the walls and ceiling! They meet about the head of Christ.

See the faces! They are turned toward the central figure.

See the hands! They point to the Christ.

The disciples look, they stare, they gesture. The gestures made by hands and arms form a line which threads its way through the groups, uniting them, and carrying straight to the central figure.

Though excited and greatly agitated, we understand that the thought of all is quickly centering about the calm figure in their midst. Here is where all the feeling of the great fresco centers!

It is said that the head of Christ is one of the most remarkable ever painted. It was never finished. The artist worked for days trying to realize his ideal. At times he would rush out upon the streets to relieve his mind of the strain.

One day he met a friend. He told him his dilemma. "Leave the Christ imperfect," advised his friend, "for you will never be able to accomplish a Saviour after such apostles."

It is true that the downcast eyes of the Christ and the unfinished head suggest all the artist could possibly have imagined the head of the Christ to be. It alone is a masterpiece.

THE ARTIST

Leonardo da Vinci was born in the little town of Vinci in Italy in 1452. Not only is he one of the world's greatest painters, but he was a poet, musician, author, sculptor, architect, engineer, and scientist. He painted the greatest pictures of the world. He built the greatest bridges of his time. He designed wonderful warships. He worked out more mechanical devices than any man that ever lived except Thomas A. Edison. He made animals that could walk, birds that could fly, and was the first to complete a model of a flying machine. This model of four hundred years ago is now in one of the museums of Europe. With all these gifts, he possessed yet another. He was remarkably handsome, and so courtly in manner that he charmed all whom he met.

As a child, music and mathematics, drawing and modeling fascinated him. When fifteen years of age he was apprenticed to Andrea del Verrochio, the sculptor of the famous equestrian statue of Colleoni.

It was about this time that the lad began to attract attention by his great beauty. Though there are no portraits of him as a youth, one biographer says: "His figure was beautifully proportioned; he usually wore a rose-colored coat and long hose, and his hair fell in luxuriant curls to his waist."

By the time da Vinci was thirty-two he had grown to be a painter and architect of renown. He was soon called to Milan, and entered the service of the princely ruler of that city. It was while in Milan that he painted his famous masterpiece, "The Last Supper."

He remained in Italy many years. Later he went to France. Here great honors were bestowed upon him. The king, Francis I, became his sincere friend. He believed that no man had ever come into the world who knew as much as Leonardo. As a mark of his esteem and friendship, he presented the artist with a beautiful chateau and a yearly income. It was here, May 2, 1519, that this great genius passed away. He died in the arms of his devoted friend, the French king.

STUDY FOR APPRECIATION

1. What is a "fresco"?
   Where is this fresco?
2. What event has the artist chosen?
   Where has he laid the scene?
   What has happened?
3. How many groups to right? To left?
   Name the disciples in each group.
4. What is the problem in arranging a
      group?
   Explain the "form" of the picture-
      pattern.
   Where is the "feeling" centered?
   How?
5. Explain how the lines of the design
      create the "center of interest."
   What can you say of the head of
      Christ?
6. Who is the artist?
   Give three other interesting facts
      about him.

Related Music: COME UNTO ME—
                  Messiah .... *Handel*
               IF WITH ALL YOUR
               HEARTS—Elijah .....
               .... *Mendelssohn*

PUVIS DE CHAVANNES
1898

GENEVIEVE SOUTENUE PAR SA PIEUSE SOLLICITADE
VEILLE SUR LA VILLE ENDORMIE

ST. GENEVIEVE WATCHING OVER PARIS
Pantheon, Paris

ARTIST: Puvis de Chavanne
SCHOOL: French
DATES: 1824-1898

ST. GENEVIEVE WATCHING OVER PARIS

In the magnificent building of the Pantheon, in Paris, is a series of mural decorations that are the pride of the French nation. Unlike the great fresco paintings of Italy these murals are modern. They were completed in 1877. They, too, are religious, but are very different from those of Italy. Instead of stories from the Bible, they tell the story of a later religious idea. They represent scenes from the life of the patron saint of Paris, St. Genevieve.

The thought of a patron saint for a city seems strange to us in America. It is, however, an idea which grew up during the Middle Ages. Every city of consequence was believed to be under the protection of a patron saint.

In view of this it is not surprising that the life of St. Genevieve found a place upon the walls of the Pantheon. Paris was her chosen city. She, in turn, was worshiped and adored by Paris.

The story of Genevieve goes far, far back to the Middle Ages. Yes, about one thousand five hundred years ago there lived in a small town not far from Paris a poor little peasant girl. Like other peasant children she tended her flocks in the field. She spent her spare time spinning, or listening to the stories of the saints. She was a good child. One day the bishop hung round her neck a coin marked with a cross. From that time on Genevieve believed herself chosen of God.

Many are the wonderful stories told of her young life. As she grew older she was more and more convinced of her calling. Persecuted, and tormented by demons, she still clung to her faith. She believed that the time would come when all Paris would know that Genevieve had been called of God. Sure enough, soon Attila, the terrible Hun, threatened the destruction of Paris. The people were ready to flee the city.

Genevieve calmed them, saying that God would protect her Christians from this pagan warrior. It proved to be true. Attila marched on. Again and again trouble and threats came to Paris, but each time the saintly Genevieve delivered her people.

By and by the people began to seek her prayers when they were afflicted. Great and many were the miracles she performed. She was adored by the French people.

Later the first Christian church of Paris was built on the site of Genevieve's home. Today she is the revered St. Genevieve. She still watches with protecting care over her beloved city.

The artist, Puvis de Chavannes, could have found no subject more dear to the French heart than the life of their beloved patron saint. Though there are many pictures in her life story, one, "St. Genevieve Watching Over Paris," is a favorite. Perhaps it is the quiet of this panel that charms all who look upon, and study this picture.

Here stands the sainted figure before the door of her home, watching over the sleeping roofs of her city. In the distance are the cool blue waters. The lone moon hangs above. Paris sleeps. St. Genevieve watches.

She stands, a simple erect figure, in a flowing robe of softened hue. The warmth of a light mantle covers her head and falls in pretty folds about her shoulders. She is alone. The moon casts its light upon the sleeping city. Shadows whisper. Inside, the oil-lamp glows. What serenity accompanies the night!

How has the artist made the picture so still? How has the artist made Paris sleep, and St. Genevieve watch? Ah, yes, that is the *art* of the picture! When we understand the art of a picture we begin to appreciate its beauty.

The artist gave much thought to his composition. He thought much about the division of horizontal picture-space. See the sky, the sea, the mass of red roofs, the wall, the pavement! Do you notice that each varies; that no two are alike? The difference is not very great. It is very subtle.

Do you notice how the tall support of the doorway breaks the vertical space? Would you move this support to the left? Would you move it to the right? Suppose Genevieve sat, as she looked o'er the city. Suppose she leaned far out on the wall. Would you like it better? Perhaps the moon could be lowered. Perhaps it could shift to the right? Perhaps it could shift to the left? And there is the beautiful jar with its delicate flower-like tree! Would a trailing meandering vine be lovelier?

Ah, the painter knew the secrets of his art! Not for one moment could Genevieve lean upon the wall. Not for one moment could the moon shift. Not for one moment could the rose tree turn to a vine.

These tall straight effects were deliberately chosen by the artist. He understood the quiet strength in tall vertical lines. He understood the repose in broad horizontal effects. He combined the two. He produced a picture of strength and serene repose. Paris sleeps. St. Genevieve watches.

See the turreted towers of the Middle Ages! See the red tile roofs! What a pretty pattern of color they make in the little space! All these colors are repeated over and over again in the picture. The distant turrets take over the delicate hue of St. Genevieve's house. The tile roof is echoed in the distant patches of the sleeping city. The moon sends a warm reflection to the city wall. It throws a cool blue shadow with clear-cut edges across the pavement. The whole scene is hushed in the serene light of night. The artist, in a perfect composition of line, form, and color, whispers the protecting care of this beloved figure. Paris sleeps. St. Genevieve watches.

THE ARTIST

The celebrated French mural painter, M. Puvis de Chavannes, early in his career passed through the disheartening experience that came to so many of his fellow artists. Like them he was ridiculed because he attempted something different. People considered him fantastic and visionary. Like Corot, Millet, and Rembrandt, he, too, met defeat.

It was not until the artist was close to thirty-five years of age that he realized he was highly gifted as a mural painter. Traveling as a young man in Italy, he had been fascinated with the work of the great Italian masters. He came home determined to become an artist. He found, however, that dreaming of an artist's career and actually realizing the dream were very different. He entered one of the popular studios, but soon became discouraged and gave up the work. Later, however, a second trip to Italy revived his desire to paint. He returned to France, set up a studio, and began his study anew. Instead of working under a master, however, he opened a studio of his own. After the fashion of the day he organized a group of congenial students for joint study and mutual criticism. Together they worked in the studio for years. Through kindly criticism and long talks about art they taught each other many things.

It was a long, long time before public notice came to him. For years he worked hard and exhibited his pictures. People went to the exhibitions only to laugh at his paintings. He met repeated rebuffs and ridicule with great patience. At length the mural paintings which he exhibited in 1861 were accepted. This was the turning point of his career. Henceforth he directed his attention to mural decoration. Today he stands upon a pedestal too lofty for criticism. The whole world recognizes him as a master in decorative art. His series of mural paintings in the Pantheon is his crowning achievement. Among these, "St. Genevieve Watching over Paris" is the most beloved.

In these famous frescoes the artist has carried out his idea of just what a mural decoration should be. He keeps as simple as possible the contrast between picture and wall. Never does he permit extremes of light and shade. Never are his figures boisterous and gay. He held that a wall, especially that of a public building, should be restful and quiet.

His pictures have a flatness of effect, for two reasons. First, they are painted in quiet delicate tints, rather than in strong contrast of light and dark; second, in the background all detail is omitted, and the color kept quiet in tone. In this way the artist gives to his wall-picture a majestic simplicity which makes it one with the wall which it decorates, rather than "a picture on a wall."

A wall must remain a wall! It must retain its structural nature in the building of which it is a part! This was the new idea which Puvis de Chavannes brought to the world.

Today the world acknowledges that the French master was right.

America is proud to possess a series of mural paintings by this gifted French artist. In the Boston Public Library he has left to this country a worthy example of his art in the decorations of the grand staircase.

Here again is the characteristic style of the artist. Everything is simple. Everything is quiet. Everything is majestic. The decoration keeps its place, one with the wall; the wall keeps its structural quality. These murals, begun in 1895, were finished in 1897.

Today the world gives to Puvis de Chavannes a foremost place among artists of the nineteenth century.

STUDY FOR APPRECIATION

1. Do you like this picture? Why?
2. Who was St. Genevieve?
   When did she live?
   Why was she beloved by the French people?
3. What time is represented?
   How is repose suggested?
4. Name the horizontal masses.
   Name the vertical masses.
   Explain the picture composition.
5. How has the artist secured simplicity?
   Name the colors and values used in sky, sea, shadows, roofs, column.
6. Point out where color is repeated.
   What quality does this give to a picture?
7. Who is the artist?
8. What was his idea of a mural decoration?

Related Music: THROUGH THE SILENT
NIGHT .... *Rachmaninoff*
NOCTURNE E ..... *Chopin*

THE FIGHTING TÉMÉRAIRE
National Gallery, London

ARTIST: Joseph Mallord William Turner
SCHOOL: English
DATES: 1775-1851

THE FIGHTING TÉMÉRAIRE

Now the sunset breezes shiver,
Téméraire! Téméraire!
And she's fading down the river,
Téméraire! Téméraire!
And she's fading down the river,
But in England's song forever
She's the fighting Téméraire.

—HENRY NEWBOLT,
The Fighting Téméraire.

The Fighting Téméraire holds forever a tender place in the affections of all Englishmen. Indeed, this old historic war ship means to the English just as much as *Old Ironsides* means to an American.

The Téméraire, meaning *One Who Dares*, was a line-of-battle ship. It carried 98 guns. It had been captured from the French in the battle of the Nile in 1798. In 1805 it took a gallant part in its last fight, the great Battle of Trafalgar.

The Emperor Napoleon had organized a great navy with the purpose of invading England. The liberty and independence of Great Britain were at stake. The defeat of his navy at Trafalgar blasted forever Napoleon's hope of conquering England.

The two fleets were drawn up for battle just off Cape Trafalgar, on the southwest coast of Spain. Soon the English ships began to move ahead. The Téméraire was second in line, leading the English fleet. Onward they moved. The signal of their great commander, Lord Nelson, in the ship ahead thrilled every loyal heart, "England expects every man to do his duty."

For hours the battle raged. The tide ebbed and turned in this great struggle of English history. The commander, the gallant Nelson, lost his life. His ship was shattered. The Téméraire moved up to the rescue.

At last the hour of victory! Above the wreck of battle, her masts and yards shot away, the head of her rudder gone, her rigging cut to pieces, towered the old Téméraire, the glory of Trafalgar's victory!

No wonder the old ship has remained the pride of the English nation!

No wonder, "in England's song forever she's the fighting Téméraire!"

This was the last fight of the historic old vessel. She was towed back to England, the pride of the English nation.

By and by, however, it was decided that the grim old warship must be broken up.

It was late afternoon toward sunset. The English painter William Turner, and a friend were rowing down the Thames toward Greenwich. The sinking sun threw a mass of golden light, ablaze with red, up over the sky. A path was reflected in gorgeous color over the smooth surface of the river.

The two men looked in admiring wonder. Suddenly out of the twilight appeared a specterlike shape! It was the towering Téméraire! It was being towed to its last berth by a fiery, puffing little steam-tug!

The two men sat breathless. Finally, "There's a fine subject, Turner," said the friend. This was in 1838. The next year our picture, "The Fighting Téméraire," was exhibited in London. Today it is considered the greatest work of that famous English painter, Joseph Mallord William Turner.

See the tall masts and high hollow bulk of the old warship! It seems a ghost,—a phantom of the past! Beside it the little tug, so much alive, is snorting and puffing as it pulls the old hero to its last moorings.

The one is so business-like, so energetic; the other, though deserted, so stately as it proudly bears its tall masts even to death.

How quiet the hour! The quietness of the scene is made impressive by the long horizontal line of the distance, and the calm, unruffled surface of the water. Two tiny men in a row-boat at the right make us feel the vastness of the sky and the solitude.

Slowly the boats draw nearer. We are quite conscious that they are moving. The long line of smoke from the tug, and the faint wake behind the old warship indicate a forward movement.

See how the eye follows this forward movement! First, the little white sail in the distance; then, the second white sail; next, the flag pole, the two masts, the line of smoke from the little tug, and on to the buoy at the right.

They move, slowly, but surely to the London wharf!

See the long dark shadows and reflections in the water. They move with the two boats, solemn and undisturbed. The long lines of the reflected masts lead up to the masts themselves, then over to the sunset sky, ablaze with color.

And the golden light penetrates to every part of the canvas! It harmonizes all the colors. It shines brightest upon the grim old warship. It lights up its faded glories. It shines on the little steam tug beside it. Here is the strongest contrast of dark and light. Thus the artist emphasizes his "center of interest."

It was the pathetic sight of this old dismantled hero of Trafalgar being towed to her last resting place that touched the heart of the English painter.

Yes, even as the brilliant lights of the sunset were fading away, so the glorious day of the old Téméraire was ending.

There's a far bell ringing
At the setting of the sun
And a phantom voice is singing
Of the great days done.

There's a far bell ringing
And a phantom voice is singing
Of renown forever clinging
To the great days done.

Now the sunset breezes shiver,
   Téméraire! Téméraire!
And she's fading down the river,
   Téméraire! Téméraire!

THE ARTIST

Joseph Mallord William Turner is one of the great artists of the world. His greatness lies chiefly in his originality, and in his use of color.

Mr. Turner was born in Chelsea, a suburb of London, in 1775. His father was a barber of Chelsea, good-natured and thrifty. He was very proud of his little son, and eager that he should grow up and become a "worthy barber."

When the child was very young he began to show talent for drawing. His drawings of birds and trees particularly attracted attention.

He liked to paint, too. One day, so the story goes, he used his father's barber-brushes to brush in a childish fancy, no doubt big and broad. Next day his father was amazed to see the lather on his customer's face turn a rosy red!

The ambitious father watched the

child's talent grow. By and by he tacked up some of the little fellow's paintings upon the wall of his shop. To his amazement, they sold! Yes, little William's pictures really sold! Ah, that meant much to the fond parents.

When the boy was a lad of only twelve he was sent to London to study. Later at fifteen he entered the Royal Academy. When he was seventeen he was employed as illustrator on one of the London magazines. At twenty-one he opened a small studio and took pupils. This, however, was too confining for his taste, and by and by we find him moving about to various places in England, always studying earnestly.

By the time he was thirty-five he was famous.

Though Mr. Turner became very wealthy by the sale of his engravings and illustrations, he was exceedingly modest and retiring in his life. Display was most distasteful to him. He was wrapped up in his art. He called his pictures his "children" and was reluctant to part with any one of them. "The Fighting Téméraire Tugged to Her Last Berth to be Broken Up," as he named this celebrated painting, was his most beloved picture. Although offered a fabulous sum, he refused to part with it. After his death it was found that he had bequeathed it to the British nation. It now hangs in the National Gallery in London.

Many are the noble deeds recorded of this famous painter. Once, upon the death of a poor drawing master, he advanced money to the family until the amount had grown to a large sum. The widow saved until she had accumulated the full amount. Then, going to the artist she made known her errand, Turner refused to accept it, saying, "Keep it, and send your children to church and to school."

Another time he sent an unfortunate beggar from his door. Then, relenting, he quickly ran down the street, called to her, and gave her a five-pound note.

Walter Scott and Mr. Turner were very close friends, the one a painter, the other a novelist. Strange to say, however, each admitted that he did not appreciate the art of the other.

"As for your books," said Turner, "the covers are very pretty."

"Well," says Scott, "I cannot see why anyone would buy Turner's pictures."

It is true that Turner's style in painting was not understood. His canvases were so alive with color, and seemed to show so little drawing, that he was openly abused by the critics of the day.

By and by one of the famous art critics came to Turner's rescue. This was John Ruskin.

Ruskin wrote many pages in praise of Turner's work. He showed how skilled he was in drawing, and pointed out that his able use of color sometimes covered up the details of drawing.

Today the whole world supports John Ruskin in all he says of Mr. Turner.

STUDY FOR APPRECIATION

1. What in this scene appealed most to the artist?
2. Did he picture his impression of the scene, or an accurate copy of it?
   What associations does it recall?
   What does Téméraire mean?
3. For what is the vessel famous?
4. What portion of the picture is sky? Water?
   What gives quietness? Vastness? Loneliness?
5. What gives dignity to the Téméraire?
   What gives movement to the boats?
6. What relation does the setting sun have to the subject?
   What unifies all the color?
7. Who is the artist?
   Where did he live? When?
8. Where does our picture hang?
   Do you like it? Why?

Related Music: DEAD MARCH FROM
SAUL ......*Mendelssohn*
FUNERAL MARCH.*Chopin*

VICTORY OF SAMOTHRACE
Louvre, Paris

SCULPTOR: Unknown
SCHOOL: Greek Sculpture
DATES: 2nd Century BC

THE VICTORY OF SAMOTHRACE

Long, long ago, in centuries past, the most beautiful land in all the world lay far across the ocean. It bordered the blue Aegean Sea. Here and there beyond the shores of the mainland, were scattered her neighboring islands. Upon the violet-crowned hills rose the marble temples of gods and goddesses. Within her cities stood glorious monuments erected to her heroes. Yes, this was the land of heroes. This was the land of the gallant Greeks of old!

Today, we of the twentieth century marvel at the beauty of these ancient monuments. We are perhaps surprised to find that the people living over two thousand years ago had thoughts in common with us of today. They too had their war memorials. They too took civic pride in the beauty of these monuments, commemorating as they did the bravery of their warriors.

The Greeks, however, attributed all

good fortune to the great gods and goddesses who, they believed, directed the affairs of the Greek world. Though they praised their warriors, their generals, their statesmen, yet they believed it was first of all to Nike, the Goddess of Victory, that they owed their great successes. Their imagination pictured Nike as a winged goddess, powerful alike on land and sea.

One day, long ago, in 306 B. C., the Greek leader, Demetrius, returned from a great and victorious sea fight off Salamis in the Island of Cyprus. His followers applauded him. He was acclaimed a hero.

This notable event must be commemorated! It must be proclaimed to all future generations! It was fitting that a statue of Nike, the goddess of all victories, should serve as a memorial to his glory.

As a result, the celebrated Nike, the Victory of Samothrace, was set up on the Island of Samothrace.

Samothrace was a sacred island with high rocky cliffs, windswept by the sea. Here on either slope of a deep ravine were the glorious temples of gods and goddesses. Here in this sacred place the great monuments of victory were raised. High up at one end of the valley stood a beautiful porch of marble columns. There, overlooking the ravine, towering above the temples and standing out against the mass of slender columns, stood the stormy wind-swept figure of Nike.

There she stood, heralding to all the world her victorious power in the great naval battle.

What an inspiration! How the sight of the glorious Nike thrilled the hearts of the ancient Greeks!

Years passed. Then came the crushing power of the Romans, and later centuries of disorder and destructive warfare. Cities were pillaged. Towns were destroyed. Temples, statues, and memorials, alike, were heaped in the dust. The Victory of Samothrace met its fate with the rest. There it lay overthrown and broken, buried for ages under the debris of the sacred valley.

In 1865 came the explorer! Two years later, digging deep into the accumulated rubbish, by long and patient exploration he discovered, piece by piece, the marble fragments of the Nike. One hundred and eighteen pieces were recovered. They were carefully collected and sent to Paris. Ten years later the pedestal, which represented the prow of a ship, was discovered. This was in twenty-three fragments. Though some of these weighed more than two tons, they, also, were sent to Paris.

Here, under trained experts, the fragments of the figure and of the pedestal were pieced together again. The head, arms, and a few other parts have never been found. The lack of these, however, in no way detracts from the beauty of the glorious figure.

Strangely enough coins of this period have also been found, which bear on the obverse side a design of this statue of Nike. These were doubtless struck as a further tribute to the victorious Demetrius. It was this ancient coin which gave the clue for restoring the Victory of Samothrace.

The design on the coin represents a figure of victory standing upon the prow of a vessel. With her right hand she holds a long straight trumpet to her lips, heralding victory. In her left she carries a trophy.

With this tiny design of a Nike serving as a guide, the skilled restorers set about the work of reconstructing the statue. Their efforts have been crowned with success.

Here stands the colossal figure, towering up more than double life size above the pedestal. Her great wings are half spread. She leads her fleet to victory. She stands erect, chest high, as she is carried rapidly forward against the wind. She triumphantly announces with a great blast of her trumpet the victory of her gallant troops!

See the windswept drapery! It clings to the figure in front. It swishes and rolls out in great folds at the back. On she goes against the breeze! On she goes proclaiming forever the valor of her mighty men,—"the glory that was Greece"!

Today this marvelous work of twenty-three hundred years ago stands in an imposing position at the head of the grand stairway of the Louvre, the great art gallery of Paris. Here the rhythmic lines of the figure are seen to advantage. The long lines of the drapery clinging in front form swinging curves of beauty as they fall to the feet. These are repeated in the rhythmic swing of the shorter garment. The high curve of the wing, carried over the front of the figure and then down and back following the line of the leg, is a line of power, giving to the figure the rush of forward movement.

Though today the artist who carved the "Victory of Samothrace" is unknown, and unsung, the world of the twentieth century pauses before the figure in admiring wonder.

STUDY FOR APPRECIATION

1. What is a "War Memorial"?

2. What does the "Victory of Samothrace" commemorate?
   Where was it found? When? In what condition?

3. When was the pedestal found? In what condition?
   What caused this?
   Where were all fragments sent? Why?

4. To whom did the Greeks attribute all victories?
   How did they picture this goddess?

5. Where is the Island of Samothrace?
   Describe its coastline.
   Why was the "Victory" placed here?
   Describe its position.

6. How were the restorers aided in their work?
   Describe the design which guided them.

7. Describe the monument as it now stands.
   Give points of beauty.
   How old is it?
   Where does it stand today?

8. Tell something of the land and people whence it came.

Related Music: POMP AND CIRCUM-
              STANCE ....*Elgar*
              TRIUMPHAL MARCH—
              Aida ....*Verdi*

PRONUNCIATION OF PROPER NAMES

COLLEONI .... (cŏl ē ō′ nĭ)

COTOPAXI ...... (kō tō păks′ ĭ)

CHAVANNES, PUVIS de ....
...... (pŭ vā′ dŭ shŭ văn)

DEMETRIUS .... (dē mē′ trē ŭs)

HASSEM, CHILDE ....
.... (chīld hăs′ ăm)

LEYDEN .... (lī den)

LYME .... (līm)

NIKE .... (nī′ ke)

REMBRANDT van RIJN ....
.... (rĕm bränt văn rīn)

SALAMIS .... (săl′ ă mĭs)

SAMOTHRACE ... (săm′ ō thrās)

TRAFALGAR .. (trăf ăl gär′,
or more commonly, tră făl′ gẽr)

TÉMERAIRE ...... (tām′ ā′ rär′)

VINCI, LEONARDO da .....
... (lē ō när′ dō dā vēn′ chē)

QUITO .... (kē′ to)

ZORN, ANDERS .. (ăn dẽrz tzôrn)

SUGGESTIONS TO TEACHERS

STUDYING THE PICTURE. Any picture presented for study becomes more interesting when freely discussed in a natural way by the class. Before reading the text it is always advisable to study the picture. Pupils should be encouraged to give their own impressions; tell what they like in a picture, and WHY they like it.

In the intermediate and grammar grades simple elements in picture-making may be pointed out,—i.e. light and shade, repetition of line, of color, color harmony, balance, and center of interest. Such questions as,—From what direction does the light come? Where does it shine brightest?—and others of a similar nature, may help the pupil to SEE. Led by the teacher's skillful questioning, pupils gradually acquire the ability to discover for themselves many elements of design in picture-making.

DRAMATIZATION. Many of the pictures used in the intermediate and grammar grades lend themselves to dramatization. Under no circumstances is it necessary to burden oneself, in the class room, with an exact reproduction. The details of costume are not required. Any outstanding accessory of dress, easily at hand, may, however, add interest. It is the pose of the figure, the grouping if there are several, and the action, that are best appreciated by the pupils when the effort is made to reproduce a picture.

CORRELATION. Many of the famous pictures of this series bear directly upon interesting historical events. These, in particular, furnish subjects for language and composition.

Drawing lessons may with real profit be given over to the tracing of pictures, for the purpose of tracing line, composition, light, and shade.

The music hour offers still another opportunity for related study. Pictures, like music, create emotions. When possible in the study of pictures, add the music which suggests the spirit and atmosphere of the picture. THE INTEREST IS ALWAYS KEENLY STIMULATED WHEN PORTIONS FROM VARIOUS SELECTIONS ARE PLAYED, AND THE CHILDREN PERMITTED TO CHOOSE THE ONE BEST SUITED TO THE PICTURE.

The suggestions for musical renderings, which follow the questions on the picture, will be of great value to the teacher.

As far as possible, each pupil should own his own pictures. This leads to the making of picture-study books, envelopes, and folders, for preserving his pictures.

STUDY OF ARTISTS. Many times when studying an artist, children are delighted to bring to the class room other reproductions of his pictures. This always stimulates interest. With several pictures by the same artist before the class, the outstanding characteristics of the painter, whether in color, composition, or some other phase of picture-making, may be intelligently discussed by the pupils. After such study as this, what "Millet" or "Rembrandt" will not be instantly recognized!

Sometimes pictures of the same subject, by different artists, form an equally interesting study. Such a series under a general subject,—as "Knighthood," "Trees," "Boats," "Joan of Arc,"—affords many opportunities for valuable comparisons. Children will readily discover that each of the artists, treating the same subject, tells his story in a different way. This cultivates intelligent SEEING, and appreciation.

Free discussion and pictures before the class are always vital to real enjoyment of the masterpieces.

To be introduced in early years to the masterpieces of the ages, and to learn of the kingly minds who have ruled in this realm of beauty, is sure to develop an interest which will enlarge, enrich, and refine the future life of the pupil.

www.ingramcontent.com/pod-product-compliance
Lightning Source LLC
Chambersburg PA
CBHW041718090426
42739CB00018B/3471